this book
belongs to:

_____

_____

_____

Sweet Dreams & Soul Truths: *rediscovering purpose in our childhood dreams* is a work of my own creation.

The information in this book was correct at the time of publication, and the Author does not assume any liability for loss or damage caused by errors or omissions, again, this is my perspective, opinion, and experience, so it has been written as such.

ISBN - 978-1-961185-79-1

Cover, Book Design, and Layout by megs thompson
megswrites llc - _www.megswrites.com_

www.inomniaparatuspublishing.com

hello my fellow dreamer,

If we haven't met yet, I'm Megs. Intuitive Writing Coach. Word-Twerking Book Doula. Ghostwriter. Editor. Publisher. All-around story sorceress.

But, before I became all that, I was just a little girl with big dreams. Wild dreams. Magical, make-believe, moonbeam dreams. I wanted to be a writer, surrounded by books, wrapped in stories & helping other people bring theirs to life.

Then, like so many of us do, I got sidetracked.

By the pressure to be practical.
By the world's expectations.
By bills and bosses & bullshit.

It took years of detours, dead ends & dark nights of the soul before I realized: those childhood dreams weren't silly. They were sacred. And yours are, too.

This journal was created to help you reconnect with the truest version of yourself—the one who existed before the world told you who you should be. Before your dreams got quieter. Before you forgot how powerful your voice is.

Inside these pages, you'll find prompts, questions & space. To remember. To reflect. To reclaim.

You don't need to have it all figured out. You don't need to write anything "the right way." You just need to show up—open-hearted, open-minded & ready to rediscover the dreams your younger self whispered before bed.

Use this journal however you need. Scribble in the margins. Answer the questions out loud. Doodle, cry, laugh, rage. This isn't about writing a perfect story—it's about reconnecting with your real one.

Give yourself 10 minutes a week—or whenever your soul feels stirred—to explore one prompt at a time. Trust what rises. And when doubt starts to creep in *(because it will)*, come back to this:

Your story matters.
Your dreams matter.
And so do you.

feeling that spark?

If this journal stirs something deep in you—a whisper of *"maybe it's time..."*—I'd love to walk with you as you explore what's next. Whether you're dreaming about writing a book, sharing your story, or just want support uncovering the gold in your words and lived experience... Scan the QR code below & let's connect.

Happy writing & dreaming,

megs

What did you want to be when you grew up?

What toys, games & activities made you feel most free & inspired as a child?

Who were your childhood heroes or role models?

_____

_____

_____

_____

_____

_____

_____

_____

_____

_____

_____

_____

_____

_____

_____

_____

_____

_____

_____

_____

_____

If someone were to have handed you a microphone at age 8, what would you have talked about? What stories would you have told?

Describe a moment from your childhood when you felt completely yourself.

What things did your younger self know to be true?

What things were you naturally good at as a child?

What did people compliment you on as a child?

When you played pretend, what did you want to be?
(Teacher, singer, mermaid, detective?)

When did you feel the most creative? Where were you? How old were you? What were you doing? Who were you with?

If your inner child could pick your job today, what would it be? *Try not to hesitate, second-guess, or rationalize the first thoughts that come to mind.*

What activities made you feel *"in the zone"* before you knew
what that meant?

_____

_____

_____

_____

_____

_____

_____

_____

_____

_____

_____

_____

_____

_____

_____

_____

_____

_____

_____

If you could relive one *"core memory"* from your childhood,
what would it be and why?

What smells, sounds, or songs instantly take you back to the happiest times in your childhood? What experiences & activities do they bring up?

What dream(s) in life have you let go of because you were told or it was *assumed* that they were 'unrealistic?'

What things have you stopped doing, not because you didn't enjoy them, but because you thought you weren't good enough or that it was *'silly?'*

If all fear of failure & judgement were removed, what things would you try again or for the first time?

What from your childhood still lights you up right now?

If your childhood dreams had evolved with you, what might that look like now?

What creative outlets or hobbies would you love to pick back up now, as an adult?

_____

_____

_____

_____

_____

_____

_____

_____

_____

_____

_____

_____

_____

_____

_____

_____

_____

_____

_____

_____

What's a job or career path you secretly envy? Why? What is it about that position or industry that you desire?

What would your 8-year-old self say if she saw you today?

_____

_____

_____

_____

_____

_____

_____

_____

_____

_____

_____

_____

_____

_____

_____

_____

_____

_____

_____

What would a life that makes *little-you* proud look like?

How could you bring more play, joy & imagination into
your work & life?

What does '*success*' look like to you now?
Not your family, or society. You.

What would you be doing right now, if you knew you couldn't fail?

What's one thing you can do this week to honor one of your childhood dreams?

If your life were a book, what would the title be? The genre? The theme? Try your hand at writing a brief summary of how you would describe your book to a stranger.

What turning point(s) in your life have shaped who you are today? Are these shifts for the better or worse?

What's something you've lived through that other women
need to hear?

What kind of story would your younger self write about your life now?

What truths in life have you had to unlearn?

What's a message or lesson you want to leave behind?

What stories are you finally ready to tell?

If you gave a TED Talk tomorrow, what would it be about?

What do you see as being the difference between surviving your life & thriving to share your story?

_____
_____
_____
_____
_____
_____
_____
_____
_____
_____
_____
_____
_____
_____
_____
_____
_____
_____
_____
_____

If your story could change just a single life, would it be worth sharing?

Notes

Notes

Notes

Notes

Notes

Notes

Notes

Notes

Notes

Notes

Notes

interested in turning your story into something more?

let's talk.